Eight Things I Wish I'd Known About Polyamory

BEFORE I TRIED IT AND FRAKKED IT UP

Cunning Minx

Do The Work
SEATTLE, WA

Cunning Minx
Seattle, WA
www.polyweekly.com

Book Layout ©2013 BookDesignTemplates.com

Eight Things I Wish I'd Known About Polyamory/ Cunning Minx. —1st ed.

For free weekly discussions about polyamory, subscribe to the Poly Weekly podcast at www.polyweekly.com or via iTunes.

Contents

Acknowledgements

Without my former partners and current podcast, this book would not have been possible. Thanks to Graydancer and his wife for having started this journey with me, to my current partner LustyGuy and his wife Elle for their love and support, and to all listeners of the Poly Weekly podcast who called in, wrote in and shared their trials and joys over the years.

Life rewards those who move in the direction of greatest courage.

—FRANKLIN VEAUX

Introduction

Hi! I'm Minx, polyamorous kinky submissive, and I've identified as polyamorous for about 10 years. For my first poly relationship, I had access to very few poly resources, had no poly friends and made every classic poly blunder in the book. I was in my 30s and was about as experienced at poly relationships as a teenager is at handling her first crush.

As the many polys who came before me had already discovered, one's first poly relationship can be extremely disruptive to one's life, psyche and emotional state. As with any healthy relationship, however, the results can be quite rewarding: a sense of loving and being loved, inclusion, balance, happiness, excitement, security and hope. Happily, I have experienced all of those to a greater or lesser extent in most of my relationships.

In battle, they say to always tell the guy who comes after you what killed you. In the first year of my first poly relationship with a wonderful partner and his fiancée-then-wife, we hit every relationship land mine in the book. And lacking poly resources and a poly support network to address them, we blindly stumbled clumsily through each one on our own, suffering through endless emotionally draining and highly frustrating discussions. There were sleepless nights, desperate phone calls, dramatic romantic gestures, longing and despair.

The reason I am writing this little ebook is to tell you what killed us. Not what killed the relationship itself; that is all but irrelevant. But rather, this book's goal is to share what could have made that first poly relationship easier on all of us. What could have made it less of a struggle and more of an adventure. What could have reduced the gut-wrenching conflicts and existential relationship angst while providing a level playing field with communication guidelines so that we all could have understood each other as well as the nature of each conflict.

It's true that no two relationships are the same, whether monogamous, non-monogamous or some brand of polyamorous. What works for me might not work for you. However, after a couple of detailed poly relationship autopsies, I can share with you some universal truths that have successfully contributed to establishing healthy, long-term, drama-free relationships. And, I might add, none of these truths are unique to poly relationships; they are for the most part equally applicable to poly-mono and strictly monogamous relationships as well.

What this book isn't

This book isn't a methodical primer on polyamory. You will not find advice on selecting relationship structures; for that, I highly recommend Tristan Taormino's Opening Up. You won't find a historical or biological recounting of non-monogamy in humans and other species; for that, read Christopher Ryan's Sex at Dawn and Judith Lipton and David Barash's Myth of Monogamy. It also isn't a philosophical or spiritual explanation of the ideas behind polyamory and loving more; for that, read The Ethical Slut by Janet Hardy and Dossie Easton. And while I am kinky and have experienced polyamory within a power dynamic, this book addresses general relationship challenges without specifically delving into power dynamics. For that, read Raven Kaldera's Power Circuits: Polyamory in a Power Dynamic.

What this book is

Instead, what this ebook seeks to do is highlight some of the classic relationship land mines that practitioners experience in poly relationships, whether it be the first time or the tenth, and offer tools and solutions to stave off those disastrous phenomena.

Who should read this book

You should read this book if you:

- are PIP (poly in principle) but either you or your partner haven't yet experienced falling in love with a new partner while still maintaining your existing relationship
- have made a few attempts at polyamory but were unhappy with the results
- In your first poly relationship now

- have made one or more attempts at a poly relationship and want to give yourself the best chance of success
- do not self-identify as polyamorous and are curious about what to expect in a poly relationship
- have a partner who has suggested polyamory and you have fears or concerns
- have dated, are interested in dating or are currently dating someone(s) in an existing relationship
- self-identify as poly, but your partner self-identifies as monogamous
- have a partner who self-identifies as poly, but you self-identify as monogamous
- are monogamous and looking to improve your relationship skills
- are not currently in a relationship of any kind but are curious about different relationship structures

What you will gain from this book

"There is no one right way to do polyamory, but there are plenty of wrong ways," quoth the wise Miss Poly Manners. While no one can tell you exactly how to structure or conduct any relationship, it is my hope that you will use this ebook as a tool for self-exploration and self-discovery. The tips and advice given here are aimed at increasing self-awareness of emotional needs with the goal of creating ongoing, transparent communication. The healthiest relationships are those in which all participants feel free to ask for what they want, hear what others want and conscientiously and compassionately negotiate to fill those wants.

Whether a current relationship continues, changes or ends, what is most important is the health, happiness and personal growth of the participants in that relationship. As my cohost LustyGuy repeats, "The goal of any relationship is to make the people involved better versions of themselves."

That's the goal I share with you. Read this ebook, do some self-discovery, and leverage your relationship to become a better version of yourself.

DISCOVERY ONE

The only "right" way to do polyamory is the way that works for you

When I made my first essay into polyamory, I did not have a wealth of resources at my fingertips. In fact, I had exactly two: Susie Bright's audio Non-Monogamy Blowout for 2001, during which she recommended The Ethical Slut.

What was frustrating about the "Non-Monogamy Blowout" was Bright's steadfast refusal to tell others what rules they should apply or how to structure their poly relationships. And, of course, she was absolutely correct in doing so: no one can tell you what is going to work for your relationship. However, it surely would have been nice to have *some* idea of what others do or perhaps a few examples to evaluate! (For a list of research on non-monogamous relationship structures and how others have customized them, refer to Taormino's book, Opening Up.) Likewise, I found *The Ethical Slut* a fascinating approach to the philosophy of loving more but devoid of any type of practical roadmap or formatting suggestions for relationship structures and guidelines.

My first mistake

So, in the absence of any poly friends or connection to a poly community, I dove into my first poly relationship headfirst, convinced that it would flame and burn within a month. When I met Gary, he was three months away from marrying June. Things actually went surprisingly well at first, considering that they were 200 miles away, and this was the first long-term poly relationship for all of us.

However, as time wore on and it became more and more apparent that Gary and I were falling in love, the tenor shifted. Communication with my metamour (the partner of a partner with whom one doesn't share a romantic relationship) became an issue. June, always fairly introverted, became less overtly supportive and increasingly silent. We repeatedly bumped into issues stemming from a lack of open communication between June and me. I made the fatal mistake of trying too hard, which served only to make her even less inclined to accommodate my requests for communication.

So what did I do? I set out to convince June that open communication with one's metamour was the *right* way to do polyamory. I constructed an online poll about the ideal state of metamour communications and sent it out to my circle of several hundred friends, hoping to gather data points to prove that I was right. Not surprisingly, the data I gathered by and large did support my beliefs.

What was wrong with this approach? Everything! The point was not whether I was right or wrong about polyamory in general; the point was that in order to be happy and healthy in a polyamorous relationship, I personally require good, open communications with my metamours. Me. Minx. Not everyone. Just me. In THIS relationship. By focusing on the "right" way to do poly rather than asking for what I personally needed to be happy and healthy in the relationship, I guaranteed its end.

The takeaway

Plenty of folks have poly relationships that don't involve ongoing metamour communications. What I learned from this extremely painful situation was that it doesn't matter one bit what the "right" way to do poly might be. It's unlikely that anyone other than you can tell you what will work for you with 100% accuracy. What matters more in terms of a relationship's success is that everyone involved must know what they want, ask for it and openly and compassionately negotiate a way to get it.

Over time, I have learned that for me, the ability to have ongoing metamour communications is essential, and the lack of that ability is a deal-breaker, no matter how much I like her partner. I have learned that if the metamour isn't open to communicate with me, I must walk away from the relationship because it will be impossible for me to be truly happy under that circumstance, even if everything else is perfect. . However, your mileage may vary—you may have entirely different needs from me. And the best way to ensure your relationship success is to know what those needs are and voice them.

Poly is a custom job

Over nearly 10 years of hosting and producing the Poly Weekly podcast, I have had the honor of having thousands of listeners share their relationship structures, challenges, joys and woes with me. And one of the key things I've learned from your emails, comments and queries is that experience is that *every* relationship is different. Every single one.

I'm convinced that if you interviewed a hundred monogamous couples about their relationships, you would discover a hundred different relationship configurations. Whether monogamous, polyamorous or some other brand of open or non-monogamous, *every* relationship is just a little bit different. One size does not fit all.

Think about it—was your first relationship exactly like your second, even though you were the same person? Is your relationship now exactly like any other that you have had? There are undoubtedly similarities and most likely a pattern or two that surface, but each one is different.

Put another way, each relationship is a do-it-yourself, custom job. That's why it's important to talk about exactly what the structure, configuration and guidelines might be rather than making assumptions about what polyamory (or monogamy or anything else) is supposed to look and feel like. So the question is not, "what are the rules of polyamory?" but rather "what type of relationship works for me/us?"

To that end, consider the following questions to ask yourself and, if you have a partner(s), discuss with him, her or them. And keep in mind that these questions should be revisited during your regular relationship check-ins over time, since our experiences sometimes change our desires, needs and values.

- What does "family" mean to me?
- What do I need to feel loved?
- What do I need to feel secure?
- What do I need to feel supported?
- What do I have to offer my partner(s)?
- What does a good, healthy relationship look like to me?
- What does "sex" mean to me?
- What does "BDSM play" mean to me?
- What are the things I must have in my life in order to be happy?
- Do I identify as an introvert, an extrovert or something in between?
- What is my preferred communication style?
- How do I prefer to resolve problems?

- What are some of the key points of my emotional baggage? What are the triggers, how can my partner(s) avoid them and what is the best aftercare they can give if triggered?

Write your user manual

For more tips for full disclosure of your key personality and relationship needs, you might want to consider writing your own user manual, a self-discovery activity that I highly recommend. A boilerplate for writing your own user manual is available in the Appendix.

Even if you never show the user manual to anyone else, having the self-knowledge and personal clarity to describe oneself accurately is a valuable skill that many partners will appreciate your having.

In fact, when I first asked my partner LustyGuy out on a date, he showed up wearing a black Utilikilt! I was thrilled to see my date wearing what I consider the sexiest of male couture... until I realized that he just might have run across my user manual online and read it thoroughly! Blushing, I asked him, "Did you... did you find my user manual and read it?" To which he replied, "Darlin', if a woman's willing to write down the directions, *damn straight* I'm going to follow them!"

While most people do not post their personal user manuals online for privacy reasons, several listeners have taken pen to paper (or laptop) to write their own user manuals, which they report having given to prospective dates as well as using to inform dating profiles.

Discovery One Summary

The only "right" way to do polyamory is what works for you. It's important to know what you need to be happy and healthy within a relationship, whether that relationship be monogamous or non-monogamous. Be ready and willing to describe what you want and need or, even better, write out your own user manual and share with your partner(s).

DISCOVERY TWO

Communication is a journey

Over ten years of practicing polyamory and the relationship drama that accompanied it, I discovered a key to relationship success, regardless of configuration: communication should be considered a journey, not a destination.

If you've considered polyamory or ever asked anyone for advice on a poly situation, chances are you heard the three rules of polyamory: communication, communication, communication. It's not a bad mantra, but many of us never learned good communication skills during our youth, and some of us have bad communication habits that we developed in adulthood as well. So what does good communication look like?

Unlike wedding vows, communication is not something that happens once and then is never brought up again until it's broken. Rather, to give yourself the best chance of relationship success, avoid taking communication for granted by instituting solid, ongoing communication habits, including check-ins, mini-discussions and post-mortems. And the great news is that all of these habits are effective, regardless of relationship structure. In short, this isn't Poly Communication 101 but rather Relationship Communication 101.

Relationship communication 101

Own your shit If you only gain one communication skill from reading this ebook, I would recommend it be this one. Circle it and put a big star by it. Owning your own emotional shit is a skill that is all too rarely seen in adults. And yet, the ability to do so is incredibly powerful when negotiating challenges in any type of intimate relationship.

Let's begin with a definition. For our purposes, "owning one's own shit" refers to the ability to take personal responsibility to understanding, diagnosing, analyzing and stating your emotions.

There are a few key assumptions at play in order to own your own shit. A disclaimer before we dive in: these are all barring cases that cross over into emotional or physical abuse, in which case, please seek help to extract yourself from that harmful situation. Barring extreme cases or abuse, the assumptions about behaviors that underlie owning your own shit.

What you feel is OK

In order to own your emotions, you must believe that whatever you feel is OK to feel. Whether you're experiencing jealousy, anger, mistrust, pettiness, loss, fear or white hot rage, it's imperative that you accept all those emotions—both negative and positive—as natural and acceptable. Believing that somehow it's not OK to feel negative emotions can lead to denial, blame or shame, none of which are helpful for honest communications.

Additionally, avoid telling yourself you should feel something different from your current state. We torture ourselves all the time with an interior monologue of "I should be happy now" or "I shouldn't feel jealous because I know she loves me." As Yoda might say, "Feel or do not feel. There is no 'should.'" Just accept every weird or inopportune emotion you have as part of the wonderfully complex machine that is you.

No one *makes* you feel anything

Emotions come from within each of us and are usually the result of a combination of programming, past life experiences and our own natural inclinations. Barring cases of abuse or violence, it's important to understand that your emotions are yours and yours alone. Therefore, we should avoid disempowering ourselves by blaming others for *making* us feel a certain way. In fact, why not embrace our emotions wholeheartedly? After all, that jealousy, fear or paranoia are often there as an early warning system, so it's important to listen to those emotions and honor them as your own.

Sometimes, there is pushback against the idea that emotions come from within rather than from external factors. Someone might say, "Wait. If my husband is late picking me up from work for the third time this week and I absolutely must be across town to pick up the kids by 4:00, then doesn't it make sense that he's making me annoyed and angry?"

To understand your emotions in this situation, take a step back and look at it from another point of view. There might be hundreds or thousands of other humans that, given the same situation, would respond differently. One might be amused and a little excited about teasing her husband about being late again (or, if into BDSM, punishing him for it!). Another might be relieved to have a few more minutes to make one more call before leaving the office. Yet another might fly into a blind rage and become physically violent. Still another might be downright happy, because she knows that if her husband is late picking her up, it means he probably pushed to finish his project today in order to spend more time with her tonight.

The fact that everyone doesn't react in exactly the same way to the same situation implies that our emotions are created within us, based on our past experiences. The husband didn't make our wife feel annoyed; she simply had that emotional reaction based on her worries, fears and past experiences. And that reaction of anger or annoyance is perfectly OK!

You are empowered to affect your emotions

The benefit of believing that your emotions are your own and not created exclusively by external factors is that it means you can not only understand and take responsibility for your emotions but also affect them as well.

The truth is that none of us can effectively control anyone else's actions. We can ask, beg, cajole or make rules to attempt to do so, but what we absolutely do have control over is us. I have control over how I think and act, and so do you. So let's stop trying to control others and simply focus on the one thing we are empowered to control: ourselves.

Outside of instances of extreme and sudden panic or rage, most emotions can easily be named, embraced and discussed rather than acted upon instinctively. Naming your current emotion is the first step in owning your own shit—and it's incredibly empowering. Once you understand and admit to yourself and others that you are feeling angry, betrayed, annoyed, hurt, afraid or freaked out, you can do something about it. As one listener recently commented, "Just naming the emotion out loud seems to make the situation a little easier to deal with."

In our example above, if our wife were owning her emotions, she might tell her belated husband, "Look, I am a little annoyed that you are late picking me up again because I need to pick up the kids by 4:00."

Now, there are quite a few places the conversation could go from here—acknowledgement, solutions, affirmations and so on. But what's important is that our wife simply and quickly acknowledged her emotional state to her husband, without shame or blame. THAT is owning your shit!

An example of emotional ownership

Let's consider an example of a common domestic instance that might spark a negative emotion. Bill arrives home after a long day at work and walks into the kitchen to see a massive tower of dirty dishes piled up in the sink, accompanied by an unpleasant, funky smell. Bill gets angry.

Bill could react in a number of ways: he could act on his anger and raise his voice to his partner. Or he could go passive-aggressive and set to washing the dishes himself while silently steaming that his partner didn't do the dishes as promised *again.* Or he could steer straight for a unilateral fix and decide that he would just be responsible for doing the dishes from now on.

But if Bill owns his own shit, he will take responsibility for his negative emotion and disclose it to his partner immediately. He might say, "Look, I'll admit I'm feeling grumpy right now because I didn't sleep well last night, so I'm overreacting to your putting off doing the dishes again. It does bother me when you say you'll do the dishes and then don't, but it's bothering me a lot more right now because I was pre-grumped."

What did Bill do here?

- Understood his emotion
- Named his emotion
- Considered and named other contributing factors to the emotion

What did Bill not do here?

- Blame his partner for causing his emotion
- Avoid the situation
- Devise a fix without communication

Again, from here, our friend Bill and his partner might go in a number of directions. A kiss and a "thank you for telling me that" might suffice. Or the partner might apologize or get started on the dishes immediately. Or they might begin or schedule a discussion on how to avoid this situation in the future. But the point of our example is not the solution; it is how Bill owned his own emotional shit and communicated it directly and transparently.

Let others own their shit, too

The corollary to owning your own shit is that it works best when you let others own their own shit, too. Again, we can only control ourselves; it is up to others to name, analyze and take responsibility for their emotions.

Minx's hot communication tips

Assume you are the expert on you This is a common refrain in my conversations with my partners and a good way to avoid invalidating a partner's shit-owning efforts by implying that they are wrong to feel a certain way.

Don't argue Avoid telling partners not to feel a certain way; let them own their own shit! If you must disagree, preface with, "You are the expert on you, and I respect that you feel that way. I will tell you that I don't see you that way; I see.... "

Embrace "yes, and" rather than "no, but" This is a classic communication technique that generally makes conversations flow much more easily. Rather than using "no, but... ," which can make a simple conversation feel combative, try using "yes, and..." For example, replace, "No, but you aren't passive-aggressive at all" with "Yes, and I haven't experienced any passive-aggressive behavior from you."

Respond with "thank you for telling me that" Owning your own shit is often embarrassing and hard, which is why most people don't do it. And many folks have had bad experiences with owning their own emotions in the past; perhaps a partner piled on more blame or even rewarded the person for acting like a victim rather than a responsible adult. So as a courtesy for practicing this extraordinary skill, let's thank our partner for having the courage to be self-aware and emotionally transparent.

Respond by owning your own shit. In addition to a "thank you," it's even better if you can respond by owning your own shit. Again, by naming and taking responsibility (not blame) for your own emotions and contributions, you are doing yourself and your partner a great courtesy.

How to argue

One psychologist became famous for claiming that if he heard a couple argue for 10 minutes, he could predict relationship success. His criteria were rather involved but can inexpertly be boiled down to this: do the people involved fight fair?

As with war, there are rules of engagement for relationship discussions or arguments that allow for full expressions of emotion while maintaining an attitude of respect. A summary of basic rules of engagement follows.

Use "I" statements rather than "you" statements

If you've ever been to therapy, especially couple's therapy, this will sound familiar. Rather than expressing guesses as to your partner's motivations, talk about your own feelings (remember those feelings that we own?). And form them using statements that begin with "I" rather than "you."

For example, if your partner was late picking you up from work, you might say, "I feel abandoned and annoyed when you are late picking me up. I have a tight timeline after work, and I feel like sometimes you don't respect that" rather than "You don't respect me or my time."

As you can see, owning your own emotions first is critical to being able to express negative emotions through "I" statements. This has some great benefits: first, it's empowering to own your own emotions and second, it's less likely to put your partner on the defensive and therefore more likely that a conversation can follow. It may sound academic, but saying "I feel abandoned" rather than "you are trying to replace me" can be quite powerful in moving the discussion forward in a productive manner.

Talk about behaviors, not your judgments of them

When the issue does revolve around a partner or metamour's specific behavior, it's important to address your emotions first and the partner's behavior second, all without making judgments or assumptions about what that behavior might mean. After all, you probably don't like it when other people make assumptions about what *your* behavior means, right? So let's offer our partners and metamours the same courtesy.

To address a specific behavior and how it's affecting you without making assumptions, try following these three steps:

1. Isolate the behavior
2. Define the emotions that the behavior elicited
3. Construct a "when _____ happened, I felt _____" statement

So for example, let's say that you've noticed on your last few dates that your partner will answer calls from your metamour while out with you but does not take your calls when he's out with him. Rather than saying, "you're treating me like a secondary" or "you're not treating me fairly," if we follow the steps above, we might come up with:

> *When you don't take my calls when you're out with Bill but do take his calls when you're out with me, I feel less important, like I am secondary in the hierarchy.*

The goal is to open up a discussion of behaviors. There may be good reasons why your partner takes Bill's calls: he may have a medical condition that requires immediate attention; he may have a job requirement; or there may be exceptional circumstances that require it now but won't be applicable next month.

Or it may be the case that your partner didn't think about the lack of fairness of the situation and is willing to discuss and change it to make you feel more accepted and loved. Approaching the issue in this emotion-owning, non-confrontational way can give the best chance of that conversation happening.

Listen

Challenge yourself to not only listen to what your partner is saying but to repeat it back to him. And it's a challenge because doing this simple task can feel quite difficult when you are in a vulnerable state.

Again, if you've ever been to a therapist, you might have been asked to repeat back what your partner just said in your own words. Now, you might not want to do this every time (that can be very annoying!), but when your partner is in an emotional state, it can be reassuring to hear you repeat back, "What I'm hearing you say is that you feel less important to me because I take Bill's calls while we are out. Is that right?" Sometimes, just feeling listened to and understood can create an atmosphere of trust and helps establish a basis of mutual understanding for the conversation.

No mind reading

Mind reading is not a requirement for any relationship. Don't assume that your partner does or should know what you are thinking or feeling. It's your job to tell your partner what you are thinking and feeling: just say it out loud. And if you are unsure what your partner is thinking or feeling, ask.

Be brave and bring stuff up

This one guideline has held me in good stead over many relationships: if you are afraid to say something, it means you absolutely *MUST* say that thing. Chances are that your partner already senses there is something wrong. So when you feel the first tinge of a negative emotion, be brave and bring it up.

What you bring up might be rather vague, such as, "I feel weird about your date this weekend, and I don't know why yet." Weird and unidentified is OK; trust that you'll figure it out. And bringing things up that are nebulous or scary is hard, so give yourself props for doing so.

Remember emotional aftercare

If you haven't realized it from the previous chapters, owning one's own emotions and bringing up difficult topics can be hard! So it's a good idea to be kind to our partners who are brave enough to bring things up and deal with challenging situations.

BDSM practitioners are familiar with the idea of "aftercare:" after a physical or emotional scene, the top or dom will take care of the bottom or sub (and/or vice versa) by applying blankets, touch, soothing words, water, snacks or anything else that will help the other party deal with the physical and emotional repercussions of the scene. It's not a bad idea to do this after our difficult conversations as well; both you and your partner(s) might need reassurance after dealing with a challenging emotional topic. Hugs, touch, reassurances of love or devotion can all be helpful after such a conversation.

Recap to reinforce

Additionally, once everyone involved is feeling less tender, it's not a bad idea to recap the discussion a few hours or a day later and briefly summarize what the issue was, what the resolution (if any) was and if there were any other steps to take moving forward. For example:

> *So you brought up the issue of my accepting calls from Bill during our dates but not taking your calls when I am out with him or Ellie. And I brought up that since we have kids together, we have the agreement that our phones are always on for anything related to the household or children that can't wait until I get home.*
>
> *That being said, I don't want you to feel like you can't reach me if you need to. So it's OK for you to call when I'm out, and I will take your call. This is with the understanding that we will all value everyone else's time and privacy and use our best judgment as to what is urgent and what can wait.*
>
> *Does that match what you understood from our talk?*

Discovery Two Summary

Communication isn't a one-time occurrence but rather an ongoing journey with yourself and your partner(s). Practice owning your own shit by working to understand, analyze and state your emotions. Conversely, let your partner(s) own her/his/their own shit, too. And always fight respectfully and fairly, using "I" statements and referring to behaviors rather than assumptions.

DISCOVERY THREE

Make guidelines, not rules

So you've spent a few months or years talking about polyamory in theory and are ready to take the plunge into dating. Great! If you're solo, carry on! Many couples, when comfortable with the theory of polyamory and first dipping their toes into poly waters, begin their discussions by making a series of rules. The rules are usually designed to restrict encounters for the purpose of either reducing the level of fear one or both parties may feel or to preserve the sanctity and priority of the original couple.

Some such couples' rules might include:

- No relationships or sex with any of our friends
- No relationships or sex in town, but if you're out of town, it's OK

- No relationships or sex with anyone of the opposite sex, but same sex is OK (also known as "OPP" or "One Penis Policy")
- We must always date the same person and always together (usually female and bisexual, also referred to as a "unicorn", with the original couple sometimes called the derogatory term "unicorn hunters")
- Our partner load must always be equal (you can only have a partner when I have a partner, and if I break up with mine, you must break up with yours)
- No sex in our house
- No sex in our bed
- Veto power over potential partners or both parties for any reason
- Do whatever you want with whomever you want, but I don't want to hear about it (also known as DADT or "Don't ask; don't tell")

Most of these restrictive rules are made with good intentions and with the goal of preserving the security and primacy of the original couple. However, they usually fail to do just that and in fact often serve as the impetus for the couple's demise. And the reason for that it quite simple: rules made out of fear are usually ineffective.

Rules don't address the fear

Because the majority of these restrictions come out of fear of loss of the current relationship, they don't actually deal with the issues they purport to address. Instead, they hide the fear behind a thin veneer that all too frequently fails to protect.

The truth is that if you already have an existing relationship, *of course* trying polyamory will change that relationship. Heck, even brining up the *idea* of polyamory will change the dynamic between the partners!

Just bringing up the idea of practicing polyamory will often result in fear, uncertainty and doubt (FUD) rising to the surface. And making restrictive rules is not terribly effective in addressing all that fear, uncertainty and doubt. Why? Because the FUD will still exist in the instance that the rules are not all followed. The rules don't actually address all the fears and insecurities at their base; they simply act as a bandage to cover them up.

Here, owning one's emotions is especially valuable: it gives people the opportunity to acknowledge their fear, uncertainty and doubt rather than hiding it behind a rule. Think of it this way:

> *If you have a child who tends to put off doing her homework, you can make a rule prohibiting TV or video games until the homework is done. But then you're in the position of being the enforcer of that rule: you have to check with the child every hour of the evening to confirm that the homework is done before the video games come out. And you will still have your uncertainties about whether the child actually is doing the homework or gaming the system.*
>
> *The child doesn't learn to be responsible on her own, and you become the nagging parent.*
>
> *But if instead you go to the child and ask why she isn't doing the homework, you might discover that she is actually afraid of doing math because she embarrassed that it's hard for her but seems easy*

> *for everyone else, so she puts it off. And if you ask her what could make it easier for her and encourage her to find a solution, she might ask for a tutor, a math video game or even for your help with the homework.*
>
> *Yes, this method might take more time than laying down a rule, but it removes the burden of enforcement off you and empowers the child to address her fears.*

The issue with restrictive rules made out of fear is that the fear isn't actually addressed, so it never goes away. I'm reminded of a monogamous friend who discovered her husband's stash of porn and promptly bid him destroy every last magazine. She felt that his looking at porn meant that she wasn't enough for him, and it raised insecurities within her. But even with all the porn gone out of the house, her insecurity lingered and surfaced in other ways, over and over again. His obeying her rule did nothing to alleviate her insecurity.

Let's look at a restrictive rule often imposed out of a sense of theoretical fairness: our partner load must always be equal. If I don't have a partner, you shouldn't, either. And if I break up with my partner, you must break up with yours.

If you feel inclined to make this rule, try asking yourself: why do I feel the need to make this rule? What am I afraid of?

Often, rules such as this one are made out of a sense of insecurity or exclusion. That is, "I don't want to feel left out, and I think I'll feel excluded if my partner is dating someone but I'm not." Or perhaps there is the fear of fear itself: what will I do while my partner is out on a date but I'm not?

Insecurity and fear of exclusion are common; I have them, myself. However, if you don't take the time to address them, you'll end up with a lot of rules and just as much drama and heartache. Take the time to drill down into what is actually causing the fear. Has this actually ever happened to you? Did your partner ever exclude you in the past? Maybe another partner did—a former wife, a jerky boyfriend? Or maybe it was that mean kid in fifth grade? Or a teacher who never called on you?

Another helpful technique is to complete this sentence:

> *I'm afraid if she has a girlfriend and I don't, it means _______________. And that means that she will _____________, and then I will be _______________.*

Remember, your fear is there for a reason. You won't have much success at polyamory until you nail it down and bring it out into the daylight where you have the power to address it. Whatever the reason for the fear, the best way to honor and overcome it is to drill down to that reason and acknowledge it to yourself and to your partner. Not only will that empower you to address the fear in the future, but also, simply having that conversation with your partner will help build trust.

Feeling special

Sometimes, these restrictions are applied in an attempt to assure that the original partners will feel special after new partners have been brought in. And this is a real and valid concern; if you love and value your relationship as it is now and are bracing for change, it's natural to be afraid that your uniqueness might be lost in the fray of New Relationship Energy (NRE), and you'll be left feeling like the comfortable old shoe rather than the sexy new designer heels.

For example, some partners might restrict where new partners can have sexual relations. Not in our house, for example, or not in our bed. Others might restrict the sexual activity. For example, oral or anal sex are OK, but only you and I have penis in vagina (PIV) sex. Or another common restriction is to do whatever you like, but no sleepovers; you must always wake up next to me.

Again, there is nothing wrong with wanting something just between two people that reaffirms the relationship and makes each person feel valued and special. However, it's rare that these rules actually serve that purpose. In my experience, they end with squabbles about what constitutes a "sleepover" (after 2:00 AM? 3:00? 5:00?) or what constitutes "our house" (does the porch count? In the car in front of the house? In the garage? What if you're not there?)

Again, try completing this sentence:

> *I'm afraid if he sleeps over with someone, it means _______________. And that means that he will _____________, and then I will be _______________.*

Facing your fears and acknowledging what you truly need to feel special—a hug, sweet text messages, a loving smile—is more likely to help everyone involved feel special.

I encourage you to have the confidence in yourself, your partner and your relationship to feel special without a restrictive rule. Rules can be broken, and they can change at some point. But if you put your trust in your partner and the strength of your relationship, it's far more effective than putting your faith in a rule.

A more effective approach

A more effective approach is to be brave and voice your fears. Admit your insecurities. Look your partner in the eye and say you have doubts. Acknowledge that you value what you have, and you trust each other enough to talk through it when things change. Empower yourself by acknowledging your emotional baggage, and strengthen your relationship by admitting that it is an organic thing that will change and grow as you both have new experiences. Trust yourself, each other and your relationship enough to embrace that change.

And if you can't do that, consider that you might want to hold off opening up your relationship until you can. Your best chance at having successful poly relationship is to begin with healthy and happy individuals in a healthy, happy relationship. In short, if the relationship is broken, don't add more people.

Setting guidelines, not rules

In contrast to rules, guidelines are more akin to guiding principles. They are also often more loosely defined as well as more loosely interpreted. They are the spirit rather than the letter of the law.

For example, if Gina and Terri want to open up their relationship, they might talk about what they would enjoy about polyamory and about what their personal preferences and fears are. And they might decide on a loose guideline of "partner familiarity." For Gina, this might mean that she wants to meet Terri's new partners early in the process so she can get a feel for their dynamic and open up a friendship, if the new partner is so inclined. For Terri, this might mean that she wants to hear all about Terri's dates so she can share in her NRE.

For neither does the guideline translate into a hard-and-fast rule about how familiar Terri or Gina should be with new metamours or when that should occur; it simply reinforces a preference for welcoming new partners overtly and for sharing in the joy.

Additionally, guidelines should be mutually agreed upon by all involved parties. To be effective, everyone that is or will be subject to the guidelines should have a say in their creation and evolution. And that includes new partners joining an existing relationship. Why should new partners get a say in relationship guidelines?

> **It's fair** If you got a say in creating the basic guidelines for your relationship, it's only fair to extend that same participation to a new partner joining your relationship.

It's respectful Offering a new partner the courtesy of a place to voice her needs and wants is an excellent gesture of respect and consideration.

It's an opportunity for communication As we recommended earlier, communication in relationships should happen early and often. It's a good idea to revisit relationship guidelines frequently anyway; when you're bringing on a new partner is an excellent time to do so.

It's empowering and effective If you are familiar with team and project management, one of the keys to successfully managing a team is to empower team members by asking for their ideas and suggestions and implementing any good ideas that are developed.

Not only will your team benefit from a richer field of ideas to choose from, but getting input from all members of the team creates a buy-in philosophy, which results in an increased sense of ownership and responsibility from each of the team members. The same is true for relationships: when you empower all partners, each partner becomes more invested in the health of the relationship.

But we have our guidelines set already. Why should a new person get equal say?

If you've ever had a rebellious bone in your body, you know the answer to this. Rules that are imposed as a dictum (even in a D/s setting where dictums are welcome) are often rebelled against and broken if the person they are imposed on doesn't feel he has a say in the situation. If a new partner doesn't fully buy in to the guidelines, it's more likely that he will stretch, strain or defy them at some point.

In contrast, if you take the time to discuss the guidelines with a new partner and ask for input, it's more likely that she will feel included and have more of a stake in the health and well-being of the relationships at hand. And who knows? That new partner might even have some good ideas for improving your guidelines!

How to discuss guidelines

When discussing guidelines, make sure that you are in a neutral space where everyone feels comfortable. Choose a time when everyone is well rested and healthy. The goal is to have a space where everyone feels safe to disclose needs, wants and fears in a conversational manner.

And keep the conversation broad with open-ended questions. For example:

- What do you need to feel good in this relationship?
- Do you have any deal-breaking triggers? Are they severe enough to merit a guideline, or will awareness of them be enough?
- Our relationship guidelines are ____________ and ____________. The first one we believe because of (insert story behind the philosophy). The second one

we like to have because of (insert story behind the philosophy). Do those work for you?

Just as getting buy-in from all team members on a project helps to ensure its successful implementation, having this discussion with new partners can help to ensure a drama-free relationship.

Safer sex guidelines

Safer sex guidelines should be discussed slightly differently from your relationship guidelines, since they deal with biology rather than emotional boundaries. The suggested questions to begin this discussion:

- Do you have any health issues that affect your safer sex needs?
- What are your precautions for safer sex?
- My/our precautions for safer sex are _______________.
- Where do our precautions intersect, and do we need to change them based on this information?

In general, when it comes to safer sex guidelines, the partner with the most restrictive guidelines often sets the standard for the entire group. That is, if one person only feels she needs testing every year and another feels safer with testing every six months, the logical solution is to test every six months, even if the person requesting that guideline is the newest in the relationship.

It's important for all sexually active adults to be well educated and well informed about the various sexually transmitted infections (STIs), including how they are transmitted, how they are treated and the level of physical harm associated with each so that everyone involved can make an informed decision about her own sexual health. Since many adults are unaware which STIs are transmitted through skin-to-skin contact (which would not necessarily be covered by a condom) and which are transmitted only through bodily fluids, it's your job to educate yourself.

For example, the most common STIs, HSV (herpes) and most strains of HPV are often relatively harmless to the subject but carry disproportionately negative stigmas in our society. In fact, one study showed that the infection rate of HSV-2 for women aged 45-50 in the United States is 75%, up to 80% of which are undiagnosed.[1]

And the rate of HPV infection currently stands at over 80% worldwide of all people who have sex at some point in their lives, most of whom remain asymptomatic and never suffer any negative effects. Your research may turn up slightly different numbers, but it's important to be informed of the prevalence of the most common STIs, along with their form of transmission and your own personal risk level.

STIs, like most other infections, affect each person differently. Family history, immune systems and current medications can

[1] Even Without Symptoms, Genital Herpes Can Spread, Science Friday, NPR

all play roles in the severity of infection, so a personal conversation with your physician is a necessary to supplement your online research.

If you don't already have a physician with whom you are comfortable discussing the level of risk of your sexual behavior, this is a good time to get one. Internet research is helpful and can provide a wealth of information, but keep in mind that the information available through government-sponsored websites changes based on the agenda of the current administration. Also, many sites showcase the worst-case scenarios rather than the most common ones, which can be a bit frightening!

When it comes to safer sex, since the physical, financial and emotional repercussions of unwanted pregnancy and sexually transmitted infections can be severe, an ounce of prevention is worth a pound of cure. Many a poly partner who has balked at the idea of using condoms and other barriers has in the end found the minor nuisances of frequent testing and barrier usage preferable to the guilt and other negative effects of passing on or acquiring an STI.

But we're a D/s household, and Sir sets all the rules

Without negotiation, there can be no consent. In every kinky relationship, there must be a safe space where needs, wants and fears can be discussed outside of the agreed-upon power dynamic. Even in 24/7 households, it is imperative to have a safe space where egalitarian negotiation can occur. In order to consent to household rules or guidelines, new members should have a say in their creation and evolution as well as the ability to revoke consent.

For more information, read Power Circuits by Raven Kaldera about polyamory in a power dynamic.

The power of the check-in

The best guidelines are general and will often stand up over time. However, as with communication in any relationship, it's beneficial to reevaluate guidelines on a regular basis.

Try instituting weekly or monthly relationship check-ins. Take 15 minutes—perhaps over coffee or before dinner—to check in with your partner(s). These are beneficial regardless of the relationship structure you've chosen; some of the healthiest monogamous relationships I've seen are healthy precisely because the partners check in regularly and head off any problems or challenges early.

Check-ins are also helpful because, well, life changes. *You* change, and so do your partners and the way you feel towards them. You might adopt a new lifestyle, new partner, new job or even a new religion. Your own self-identity, goals, values or life philosophy might shift over time. Sharing those changes with your partner on a regular basis can help make them far easier to handle than silence followed by an earth-shattering pronouncement.

There is a story that you might have heard about an old wife complaining to her old husband, "You never tell me you love me" and his responding with something like, "I told you I loved you when I married you. If that ever changes, I'll let you know."

While the story purports to be a sweet tale of what I suppose would be defined as the "strong but silent type," that lack of communication doesn't work terribly well for most people. Most of us need to hear "I love you" more than once in a lifetime, and most of us find it easier to deal with life changes in small, manageable bites.

What does a check-in look like? At the beginning of a new relationship, it might be an hour-long discussion. Weekly check-ins over time, however, can be as short as 5-10 minutes.

A sample check-in:

- How are you feeling about us right now?
- Are you worried about anything?
- We've been talking about ______ issue over the last few weeks. How are you feeling about that now?
- Anything you want to bring up?

If you do weekly or monthly check-ins, you'll discover that they serve as excellent points not only to check the pulse of your overall relationship health but also to reevaluate any guidelines you might have in place. Stuff changes. What was a great guideline one year might seem too restrictive or irrelevant the next. Regular check-ins are a great way to avoid the drama that comes with change.

Discovery Three Summary

Since rules made out of fear tend to be ineffective, work to confront your fears and insecurities rather than making rules to protect them. Set broad relationship guidelines rather than strict rules, and bring new partners in on the discussion for buy-in. Establish regular relationship check-ins to help with adjustments over time.

DISCOVERY FOUR

Partners are human

When it comes to polyamory, it's easy to get caught up in the pleasure of diversity (or diversion) and forget that the partners we are bringing into our lives are human beings with needs, insecurities, desires and feelings of their own. So this I encourage you to remember: *everyone* deserves to be treated with respect.

It's unfortunate that most of the advice, books, classes and sessions available on polyamory are from the point of view of a couple who has decided to open up their relationship. It's quite rare that the point of view of the solo polyamorist or the person who is entering an existing relationship is considered, although there is an excellent blog available on the subject of solo poly, which I encourage everyone to read.

Much of the information available today is directed at the couple and is focused on how to dip the toes into polyamory without damaging, threatening or changing the existing relationship.

Because this book is directed at *everyone* interested in polyamory, including couples, singles and free agents, we'll consider polyamory from all angles. That being said, this chapter in particular is directed at couples who are opening up their relationships.

Dealing with change

By the very fact of suggesting polyamory, the couple's relationship has already changed. There is probably some FUD (fear, uncertainty and doubt) involved, usually around losing what is good about the existing relationship. Sometimes, the fear is simply of change or the unknown. Those feelings are normal; everyone has experienced them at one time or another. It is practically impossible to switch from a conventional to an alternative lifestyle without some level of fear and uncertainty around the relationship.

And remember that, if the partner who agrees to date you is new to poly as well, he most likely also has his own set of fears and insecurities. When I first began dating a man who was engaged, my friends feared that I was "settling" for someone who was already taken out of a lack of self-respect. They feared I was entering a relationship with no future for me in it. They feared my position as lover to a married man was disposable. And to be honest, I was a bit afraid of that, myself. And with good reason—many couples *do* in fact treat their first few poly partners as disposable and dump them unceremoniously when their own fears and insecurities get the better of them.

I was also afraid of being seen as a "home wrecker" that would destroy a beautiful, healthy existing relationship. And as my poly journey continued, I began to fear being treated as a second-class citizen or an obstacle to the couple's happiness rather than someone who brought something beneficial to the existing relationship.

Your new partner is human and will have her own fears and insecurities, just as you do. If you're not willing to work through those with her just as she is willing to work through your insecurities with you, it's probably a good idea to wait on opening up your relationship.

But your new partners aren't playthings

Your new partners aren't your playthings (unless, of course, that dynamic is consented to by all parties involved). Neither are they threats to nor solutions for your current relationship problems. It is disgraceful how some partners are treated in the community by couples looking to fix their own dysfunctional relationships, and we should stop the practice of "relationship broken; add more people" immediately.

If you have concerns about opening up your relationship, the best path is to take the time to get secure with yourself and your current relationship first. A good rule to follow is: if you are afraid a new partner will threaten your relationship, or if you are convinced that adding a new partner will save your relationship, it's probably not a good time to open up.

Terrible reasons to try polyamory

Polyamory isn't for everyone. Not everyone self-identifies as polyamorous, and not everyone who tries polyamory determines that it is the right lifestyle choice for them. Some people are perfectly happy being monogamous; some find that monogamy with a "don't-ask-don't-tell" clause works best for them; others find that partnered non-monogamy or a brand of polyamory suit them best.

There is nothing wrong with trying polyamory on for size and determining that it's not a good fit for you. However, there is a time and place for making the essay into polyamory that will be most likely to yield positive results. So before taking the plunge, check to be sure that you don't have unresolved issues that will hinder the outcome of any new relationships. And do a quick check of your motivations. Are you trying poly for one of the following terrible reasons?

Because the current relationship is broken

The "relationship broken; add more people" model has been proven time and again to result primarily in misery, drama and heartbreak. If everyone involved in the current relationship is not already happy and healthy, hold off on trying polyamory until they are. It's unfair and unkind to put new partners through the relationship wringer of a couple airing its dirty laundry.

Fix your current relationship before adding a new one. If your current relationship is unfulfilling, involving more people won't fix it. While polyamory does provide many people with the opportunity for increased joy, it's not a cure for boredom or dissatisfaction. Heal yourself and your existing relationship before endeavoring to pursue a new one.

And as with dating monogamously, the best advice you'll ever get is to be your own best, happy, healthy self before you go out looking for new partners.

Because you can try it and revert to monogamy if it doesn't work out

This mindset is often coupled with veto power to ensure that if one partner feels threatened, the whole adventure can be called off. Not only is this veto ability unfair and unkind to anyone that you might date and who might have fallen in love with you or your partner, but it's often far more damaging when wielded than you might realize.

In almost every instance I've seen of one partner wielding veto power and reinstituting monogamy for the couple, trust is shattered and never rebuilt. Think about it: how would *you* feel if you fell in love with a wonderful person; it's going great; and a year later, your partner says you have to give him up and go back to monogamy? It's a difficult bridge to rebuild. Not impossible, but difficult.

And remember that polyamory isn't just about the couple: when you invite another person into your relationship, that person is trusting both of you with his heart. If your plan is to bail when you get scared, it's unfair to your potential partners to open up your relationship in the first place.

I would encourage those trying polyamory to consider taking on new partners with as much commitment as you would for adopting a child. This is not to say that you should cling to your first poly partner no matter what. It's quite rare for the first poly relationship to be sustainable over time; we all tend to make a mess of things the first time we do them, and the first poly relationship is no different.

However, going into your first polyamorous relationship with the understanding that you are dealing with a human being who has her own feelings, needs, wants and fears is helpful. And just as it would be unkind to return an adopted child that your partner who has fallen in love with after a few months, so too is it unkind to insist upon returning to monogamy when your partner is enjoying a loving relationship.

Because you're afraid your partner will break up with you if you don't

Some people have a fear, whether implied or explicitly stated, of losing a current partner if they aren't willing to consider opening up the relationship. It's not a good idea to make a major lifestyle change out of fear.

If the only reason you are willing to try opening up your relationship is out of explicit or implicit fear of losing that relationship, stop. Open up conversations with your partner about what you want and need and what you are afraid of. Create a safe space where you can share your emotions, your emotional baggage and your fears without blame, shame, accusations or retribution. If it's within your means, visit a counselor, alone or with your partner, to address your needs and fears.

Great reasons to try polyamory

Enough of the doom and gloom! On the other hand, there is a plethora of excellent reasons to take the plunge into non-monogamy. For all of the challenges inherent to trying an alternative relationship structure, polyamory can be extremely rewarding to those who practice it. Many couples, vees, triads, quads and polycules have found that adopting a polyamorous lifestyle is not only true to who they are but enriches their lives, their existing relationships and those around them as well. So what are the healthy reasons for exploring polyamory?

Before diving in to this section, it's important to say that anyone can try polyamory at any time. While I often refer to couples opening up their relationship as the most common model, it's not unusual for individuals young and old to self-identify as polyamorous, even if they are not currently in a romantic relationship.

Because it's being true to yourself

While this is not the place to argue whether human beings are naturally monogamous (although if you are interested in scientific research, Sex at Dawn and the Myth of Monogamy are both excellent reads on the subject), some people feel that they are "hard-wired" to be polyamorous. These people feel that polyamory is an orientation they are born with, much like being gay, and they often report that giving themselves permission to explore polyamory feels like they are being true to themselves.

Others describe polyamory as a preference or a choice and describe polyamory as a relationship structure that made more sense to them than the standard serial monogamy. Either way, choosing to explore polyamory because it feels like the most sincere expression of your natural inclinations is a great reason to self-identify as polyamorous

Because you are awesome and want to share it

Many couples have healthy and happy relationships and an inclination towards non-monogamy. Others have a curiosity about recreational sex, kink or BDSM or simply wish to experience NRE again. Solo polyamorists might have a healthy relationship with themselves and wish to enjoy what another solo polyamorist, couple or more might have to offer.

Because you want to explore new erotic or emotional experiences

As mentioned above, a curiosity about new erotic or emotional experiences and an attitude of those experiences improving both the self and (if there is one) the current partnership is healthy.

Because you want to bring new skills to your current relationship

While many first-time polyamorists fear losing what they have, there is a positive flip side: adding a new partner can bring a wealth of benefits to both the individual and the couple, including a new dynamic, new sexual skills, new fetishes or simply a new appreciation of the health of the relationship.

When LustyGuy and I started dating, none of his current relationships involved any sort of BDSM play, despite the fact that he had a background in kink. When he and I started dating, we spent some time discovering where our sexual kinks overlapped. In particular, we are both fond of rough body play, wrestling, slapping and breath play through choking.

We went on our merry way playing with these kinks during our intimate times together, and he mentioned to both his wife and his other partners what he and I were exploring. One partner in particular was curious, so they tried breath play and some rough body play during their intimate times.

The response was, "Holy crap! Thank Minx, and yes, more of that!" This is what LustyGuy refers to as "blowback."

Never underestimate the value of bringing new sexual skills back to current partners!

Discovery Four Summary

As you make your essays into polyamory, whether you are solo, a couple or more, remember that the people you are making those essays with are human beings. They deserve to be treated with respect, and that means that making sure you (and if you have one, your partner) are happy, healthy and secure before trying polyamory.

If you intend on having a safety net of clamping the relationship shut when you get scared, just think about how you would feel if someone prevented you from seeing the partner you love because she's insecure. If you wouldn't want someone to do it to you, give your new partners the same respect and consideration, and don't do it to them.

DISCOVERY FIVE

New Relationship Energy is Fun

New Relationship Energy (NRE) is that wonderful sense of euphoria people experience when they begin a relationship with someone they feel an extreme attachment to. The rose-tinted goggles go on, and life is great!

Your feet don't seem to touch the ground; you're as corny as Kansas in August and high as a flag on the Fourth of July; all the songs on the radio make sense and seem to be sung just about *you* and your newfound, earth-shattering, life-changing new love. The sky is bluer; the birds sing just for you; you go around with a ridiculous smile on your face all day long. Your new love is the center of your universe, and everything he says and does is exciting, brilliant and amazing. Every touch feels like the first; even the afterglow shines more brightly than ever before.

What is happening during this experience is that the brain is being flooded with chemicals that induce those sensations of attachment and euphoria. Oxytocin and vasopression are the primary culprits that drive attachment. Vasopression is a neurohypophysial hormone that plays a role in sexual motivation and pair bonding.

Oxytocin (also known as "the attachment hormone" or "the bonding hormone") is a neurohypophysial hormone associated with long-term attachment and is released after orgasm as well as during childbirth and lactation to facilitate mother-child bonding. The fun chemicals dopamine, norepinephrine and serotonin drive attraction but are also related to loss of appetite and sleep.

Dopamine and norepinephrine are neurotransmitters and Norepinephrine is also a stress hormone that affects the amygdala, the part of the brain associated with attention and fight-or-flight response; this is most likely why people in love become focused on their new relationship and why they become so terrified of losing it. And serotonin is a monoamine neurotransmitter associated with infatuation and the sensation of being blinded to all else.

At the hands of all these powerful chemicals, it's no wonder that NRE is so very powerful. However, whether you're solo or partnered, it's important to make sure that enjoying the love goggles doesn't ruin the rest of your life. A few tips on handling NRE:

- **Enjoy it** NRE is a wonderful experience and a happy benefit of polyamory. So enjoy the NRE with your new partner and revel in it all you like! Be all shiny and silly and full of unicorns and rainbows.

- **Share it** A benefit of polyamory is that if you are experiencing NRE and are in a current relationship, you can bring that energy home to your current partner so that your existing relationship can benefit from it as well. Let those yummy brain chemicals spill out into your existing relationships: get more down and snuggly with your husband; take your wife out dancing; try out your newfound role-playing skills with your boyfriend. Spread the love.

- **Never pack anything larger than a suitcase** A good rule of thumb is not to pack anything larger than a suitcase during NRE. Do not pack up the moving truck with all your belongings and move across town, across the state or across the country to be with your new love. Do not quit your job or change jobs.

During NRE, consider yourself to have the judgment of a teenager whose frontal lobe is not yet completely formed. Remember that if you really love this person, you'll still be in love with him in a year when the chemicals wear off and you can apply more critical thinking skills to the situation.

And if you're not still with him a year later, celebrate! You managed to save yourself the drama and trauma of a tragically impulsive life change made when the chemicals were running the show. And now you don't have to repack up the truck and move back home.

Discovery Five Summary

So please do enjoy your delicious soup of brain chemicals, and do share it with your loved ones! They'll be happy for you. Just remember they'll be less happy if you subject them to the drama of a major life change while neglecting their needs in favor of those of your shiny new lover.

DISCOVERY SIX

You don't have to do it alone

When my first poly partner Gary came out to me as polyamorous, I had never heard the word before. So when, a few months later, I acknowledged the attraction and indicated I'd be interested in dating him, I was going in to the relationship all but blind. At the time, he had a fiancée, and none of us had any idea of how to embark on this poly adventure. They had had some experience with finding a friendly third at a party of open-minded folks but had not yet experienced building a long-term relationship with a third partner.

Because of our inexperience, we stumbled through the first year or two of polyamory with many discussions, many tears, much pulling of hair and much gnashing of teeth. Eventually we did discover *The Ethical Slut*, thanks to Susie Bright's Non-Monogamy Blowout radio show, but we had no close friends who identified as polyamorous, no roadmap and no idea what we were doing, whether we were doing it right or if anyone had ever experienced what we were going through. And worst, we had no one to talk about our growing pains as we slogged through that tremendously difficult first poly relationship.

I wish I had known during that time that there were poly message boards, forums and live meetup groups where I could have talked with others who had already been through the first-time poly wringer and could have offered advice or at least sympathy. It would have been wonderful not to have gone through that in isolation, with only each other to rely on for insights.

But the great news is that you don't have to go through what I did. Today, there are a wealth of books, online groups and real life communities dedicated to discussing polyamory and sharing advice and experiences. Still other communities are devoted to socializing with others who identify as polyamorous or non-monogamous, and many offer social outings from pub crawls to camping events to potlucks to blues dancing.

Let's start with publicly available resources. Even if you live in a remote area, books, podcasts and online forums and communities are still available to you:

Polyamory 101 books

If you are exploring polyamory right now, you are blessed to be living in a time when dozens of books are available to help you with your journey. Every book listed here covers the basics, including defining polyamory and other terms, dealing with jealousy and basic relationship communications. This is by no means an exhaustive list, and with any luck, this list will be out of date quite quickly, with many more excellent resources to be published soon.

Opening Up: A Guide to Creating and Sustaining Open Relationships, by Tristan Taormino. This book is the number one, must-have read for anyone exploring any type of non-monogamy. An accessible and practical guide to the relationship structure options when exploring non-monogamy, it's based on research with over 120 subjects and covers all the basic practicalities of polyamory and open relationships. Read this one first!

The Ethical Slut by Dossie Easton and Janet Hardy. A new revision of the classic polyamory primer by two of the pioneering women of polyamory; everyone considering non-monogamy should read this to begin the thought process of loving more. And at the very least, fill out the chart in the middle.

Polyamory: the New Love Without Limits by Deborah Anapol. Another classic by a poly pioneer Deborah Anapol, who brings a California counselor's touch to the introduction. Ethics, jealousy and the basics of coming out are covered.

Pagan Polyamory: Becoming a Tribe of Hearts, by Raven Kaldera. Even if you don't self-identify as pagan, this book looks at polyamory from the point of view of real people really living it. They tell their stories and share their rituals for dealing with jealousy, bringing in new partners and even losing partners. A useful and touching read.

Polyamory: Roadmaps for the Clueless and the Hopeful, by Anthony Ravenscroft. This is a good fourth book to have on polyamory. A bit verbose and occasionally redundant, Ravenscroft takes a great, personal, ultra-pragmatic and super-opinionated approach to poly in it. The gloves are off!

Power Circuits: Polyamory in a Power Dynamic, by Raven Kaldera. Kaldera's book is the only one to address polyamory specifically in the world of BDSM, where deliberately unequal power dynamics can complicate the application of polyamory. This book is a must-read for BDSM practitioners, both tops and bottoms alike. Yes, even for the Big Domly Doms Who Know Everything.

Poly memoirs

In the last few years, several polyamorists have stepped up to write personal memoirs to share with the public rather than polyamory 101 primers. Since I'm a big believer that shared stories make us all stronger and wiser, I encourage you to pick up and read these as well.

Open: Love, Sex and Life in an Open Marriage, by Jenny Block. Jenny Block's intimately relatable memoir tells her tale of being honest about who she is and what she wants. Now a writer for Fox News and Huffington Post, Block wrote this memoir as the girl-next-door, suburban housewife telling the story of how open marriage worked for her.

Open All the Way: Confessions from My Open Marriage, by Sadie Smythe. This brutally honest memoir is a collection of stories chronicling Sadie and her husband Scott's forays into open marriage, including the bumps they hit on the road and her entertainingly intellectual support and analysis of them.

Research-based books

If you're curious about the biological, anthropological or sociological study of monogamy and non-monogamy, these books provide useful and sometimes hysterical insights.

The Myth of Monogamy, by Judith Lipton and David Barash. This book presents Lipton's and Barash's research based on new DNA fingerprinting technology that uncovered the fact that birds, once touted as biologically monogamous, in fact birth young by as many as five different mates. Find out how birds and other species (including humans) are scientifically proven to be "socially monogamous" while philandering about in extra-pair couplings.

Sex at Dawn: How We Mate, Why We Stray and What It Means for Modern Relationships, by Christopher Ryan and Cacilda Jetha. This examination of the prehistoric origins of sexual behavior is a delightfully controversial deconstruction of conventional wisdom about sex and monogamy—while still being a fun and accessible read. For a preview, Ryan's TED talk Are We Designed to Be Sexual Omnivores?

Why We Love, by Helen Fisher. Fisher, a cultural anthropologist, delves into brain chemistry and the science of attraction. Think you're the only one who's ever been in love LIKE THIS? Think again! A fascinating read, even for non-anthropologists. Want a preview? Fisher's TED talk on The Brain in Love.

Dr. Tatiana's Sex Advice to All Creation, by Olivia Judson. This witty approach to the biological nature of sexual contact in the animal kingdom is written as a Q and A to an advice columnist. Dr. Tatiana (a.k.a Judson) advises, for example, when necrophilia is acceptable, how to have a virgin birth and when it's OK to eat your lover!

Local meetups

Reading about the principles of polyamory is a great place to start. And in order to have a chance at a truly successful poly relationship, it's important to create and nurture a poly support network.

Polyamory is an alternative relationship structure. Even the most well-informed and well-intended of monogamous friends and family are unlikely to be able to offer the type of advice and support necessary during your first few attempts at polyamory. For those who have accepted monogamy as being *de rigeur,* it's difficult *not* to diagnose polyamory as the source of any and all trouble in relationships. It's imperative to surround yourself with a group of experienced polyamorous friends who can offer sympathy, advice and perspectives based on their own real-life experiences.

As you forge ahead in your poly journey, it is important to have poly-friendly connections with whom you can share your doubts, fears, joys and questions. Trying to have a polyamorous relationship without a support network is like trying to canoe upstream without a paddle: not impossible, but it requires a lot of extra effort and aggravation. So even more important than finding that perfect poly partner is finding a few good poly friends to lean on for support. And, of course, that experience is mutual: even with very little poly experience, you can provide insight and support to others as well.

If you are exploring polyamory right now, you're exceptionally fortunate to live in a highly connected world in which information and personal connections with poly-friendly people are only a quick Internet search away. It used to be that the only way to seek a poly partner was to place an ad in the back of the local alternative newspaper or magazine and hope for a response. And it was nearly impossible to find like-minded polys to chat with about the lifestyle outside of pagan circles. Today, however, real people meet every day all around the world to eat, drink, chat and share their poly experiences with friends and strangers.

How to find a local meetup

I'm often asked if I know of any meetups in [city name]. Since meetups and groups tend to grow, change and fade organically over time, it's difficult for any one person to be constantly up to date. The easiest way to discover poly groups in your area is to search online first. Just type your city/area name and the word "polyamory" to find what poly groups already exist nearby. Also, the Poly in the Media blog has a page devoted to lists of local meetups.

How to attend a poly meetup

A poly meetup might be called a munch, brunch, slosh, happy hour, salon or coffee. Meetups usually occur in public or semi-public spaces and are designed to facilitate socialization in a safe environment. A few tips on attending a meetup:

- **Bring a buddy** If you're nervous about meeting a group of strangers, consider bringing a friend or a buddy along to increase your comfort level.
- **Find the organizer** Ask if you are in the right place for the poly meetup (just in case you're not!) and find the organizer. Introduce yourself and let him/her know this is your first time attending. The organizer will be happy to introduce you around and to familiarize you with any guidelines governing the event.
- **Be yourself** If you're introverted, it's OK to be quieter than the rest of the group. It's also OK to feel awkward or excited or chatty. Better to be yourself than to put up a front.
- **Introduce yourself** Be brave and introduce yourself to the folks you're sitting next to.
- **Be curious** Poly folks love to answer questions! If you don't understand a term being used, ask. If you have an issue you'd like to ask advice about, get permission

to ask for the advice first ("Is it OK if I ask your advice on a poly issue I'm having?") and then go to it.

- **Listen** If you're shy (and even if you're not), be a good listener. Most people are terrible at listening, and if you give others the chance to open up to you, you'll most likely discover some wonderful new friends.
- **Seek friends, not dates** While you may end up meeting someone at a poly meetup with which you have chemistry, keep in mind that community and connection are the most valuable benefits of the poly community. Seek to make friends rather than treating the meetup as a dating pool.
- **Pay your bill** and don't forget to leave a tip!

And a quick note: just because someone is poly doesn't necessarily mean she will be your best friend and confidante. In fact, you might not even *like* a lot of the people you meet at poly meetups! That's OK. I don't always have a lot in common with people at some of my local poly meetups, either.

As with any other group, there are always a few overly opinionated loudmouths, the creepers and the jerks. And as with the rest of life, you are within your rights to pick and choose your friends. Just go in with an open mind, and feel free to ignore the folks who turn you off. If the behavior of someone makes you especially uncomfortable, mention it to the event organizer, who has a vested interest in attendees' comfort and safety.

What if there is no meetup?

If your search turns up no results, it's possible that there are no established poly meetups in your area. And consider this: it's unlikely that you were the first person to search for a local poly meetup and be disappointed at the results. So why not start the first meetup in your area?

Starting a poly meetup

If there are no poly meetup groups in your area, you can be the first to start one! While this may sound like a daunting task, it's likely that you'll soon discover that you are not alone in your desire to have a poly community in the area. A few tips for organizing a meetup:

- **Find the right space** Select a public space, usually a coffee shop or restaurant, that can accommodate the size group you expect. Choose a central location that is accessible by car and by public transit with easy parking. Ask the owner or manager for permission for your group to meet there—keeping a good relationship with management is important. If the event is a munch, make sure that the menu is broad enough to accommodate attendees who have dietary restrictions.
- **Get a co-conspirator** Weekly or monthly events can be wearying to the organizer, so get a buddy to help shoulder the load.
- **Promote** Use social networking sites and meetup or event sites to promote your event. If there are com-

munity event calendars in your area, be sure your event is listed there. If you have a local GLBT or sex-positive center, list your on the calendar and provide fliers for distribution. Likewise, sex-positive toy shops might be willing to let you post fliers in their stores.

- **Respect privacy** As you promote your event, be aware that many folks are not out as polyamorous. Never post a photo of someone nor tag anyone on a social networking site without explicit permission. Also make it clear that privacy and, if desired, anonymity will be respected at your event.

- **Involve the community** One of the best organizing tips I ever got was to leverage the first few people to attend the event and involve them in the organization. Ask their advice moving forward, and invite them to take on responsibilities for the group as well. The goal is to move from a dictatorship to a committee. That way, when you are ill or busy, the committee can move the group forward without you. Spread out the responsibility.

- **Be patient** A few years ago, an online friend contacted me and asked me to attend his first poly discussion and meetup group in Milwaukee, held in a sex-positive toy store. He was expecting only his two partners and I might attend. Instead, over two dozen curious poly people showed up! You might not be so fortunate with your meetup; it can take months or years for meetups to build popularity. So be patient.

- **Make introductions** Be sure to assign a greeter or "cruise director" to welcome new members, make introductions and facilitate conversations at each event.
- **Avoid creepiness** While this should go without saying, it unfortunately doesn't. Don't use the meetup as a personal dating pool; avoid hitting on attendees for dates. Likewise, pull aside any members that appear to be hitting on attendees or otherwise creating uncomfortable situations. It's the organizer's responsibility to set the mood of the event and to enforce its rules to ensure everyone feels safe and comfortable.
- **Get feedback** One of the best ways to grow an event is to solicit feedback from attendees on location, genre, conversation topics, and so on.

Poly conferences

For the intellectual and the brave, there are also a variety of workshops and weekend or longer conferences devoted to polyamory and non-monogamy. Conferences can be an excellent way to get a wealth of information on polyamory from a variety of expert sources all at once. Many conferences include mixers for newbies and entertainment including concerts, cabaret, dances, speed dating or even play parties. Alan of the Polyamory in the News website keeps an updated list of major poly conferences worldwide.

Discovery Six Summary

One of the most difficult paths to polyamory is the one that is taken alone. In today's highly connected world, there is no need to make this difficult lifestyle change without help. Read books, gather wisdom, chat online and reach out to others in your area. You'll quickly discover that poly folks are always ready to offer an opinion, advice and sympathy.

DISCOVERY SEVEN

It starts with YOU

Whether you identify as polyamorous or monogamous, a top or a bottom, a dominant or a submissive, relationships don't work unless you know, understand and love yourself first. If you aren't already capable of knowing who you are, what your emotional baggage is and how to love and accept yourself, it's unlikely that your relationships of any kind will be healthy, happy and free of drama.

Take inventory

So before diving into polyamory, do a quick self-check and make sure that you are the best person you can be. Make sure you have a good handle on how you rate on these essential relationship skills:

- **A high level of self-knowledge** Self-awareness is the first step to a healthy relationship of any kind. Do you know yourself well enough to be able to understand and label the motivations behind your actions? Do you have the desire and ability to explain your needs, wants and actions to yourself and to others? Can you own your own shit?

- **The ability to ask for what you want** Are you brave enough to ask for what you want and need? Can you handle asking for what you need and not getting it?
- **The ability to hear what others need** Do you have the courage to hear what your partner or loved one wants or needs without making it about you?
- **Emotional intelligence** Do you have the ability to separate behaviors from the emotions surrounding them? For example, in a moment of anger, can you stop and describe how you are feeling and why you are feeling it rather than acting upon it?
- **The ability to embrace change** Are you willing to accept that you and your relationship will change? Even if you fear change, can you embrace it and trust that it will be for the better? Can you be flexible in the wind and bend without breaking?

You'll notice that none of the relationship skills listed above are specific to polyamory. The truth is that everything required to make a healthy poly relationship is exactly the same as what is required to make a healthy monogamous relationship: self-awareness, honesty and flexibility. And none of those skills are unique to polyamorists; many successful monogamists embrace them wholeheartedly as well.

Change

Change is important in any relationship and especially so in polyamorous ones. A new partner will almost always change the existing relationship dynamic in one way or another—and it might not be in the way you expected!

> *Recently, I got an email from a submissive woman who had taken a kink couple as lovers. They gave her one rule: she was never to tell either person she loved them. This was OK at first, since she was happy simply to be in service to both.*
>
> *You can guess what happened next. As often happens with real humans, the submissive developed feelings for one of her partners, the husband, and finally admitted her love for him. Needless to say, much emotional pain, drama and a breakup ensued.*

Dogmatic folks who make strict rules and never change them tend to get lied to, cheated on and left a lot. Healthy relationships are able sustain growth through change.

It wouldn't be honest to write this book without acknowledging that some relationships simply aren't healthy and don't work out. And from the outside, it might be easy to blame the polyamory for a relationship's untimely demise. However, from thousands of emails and conversations over the years, it's been rare to see a relationship that began healthy destroyed by opening up to polyamory. What happens more often is a relationship has miniscule cracks that haven't been addressed, and by opening up that relationship to polyamory, those cracks grow and threaten the health of the relationship.

And just as any one divorce or affair doesn't prove that monogamy is broken, one ended poly relationship doesn't prove that polyamory isn't a valid relationship model. It simply means that polyamory wasn't right for those particular people at that particular time in their lives.

Why relationships fail

So why do relationships, especially poly relationships, fail? While each relationship, poly or monogamous, is unique, the reasons for their dissolution are often all too common. And the reasons listed below are by no means unique to polyamory. A healthy relationship requires the parties involved to be self-aware, honest, brave, emotionally intelligent and good communicators in order to support a long-term, loving bond.

- **Being untrue to oneself** A primary reason relationships fall apart is because one or more of the people in the relationship aren't being true to themselves. It's quite common for a partner to hide a deep desire, need or self-identity. Over years, that secret can create emotional distance, leading to an eventual rift. Likewise, some folks make either a tacit or explicit sacrifice for a partner that can seem too great over time if the sacrifice involves giving up a part of their self-identity.

- **Lack of communication skills** Basic communication skills such as active listening, communicating one's own needs clearly, expressing empathy and arguing respectfully and fairly are essential for maintaining healthy, loving relationships. However, many folks have difficulty communicating honestly within intimate relationships, which can lead to assumptions, implications, inferences and eventually, the end of the relationship.

- **Lack of emotional intelligence** Good relationships start with good communication, and good communication starts with a high level of self-awareness. As mentioned in Discovery Seven, emotional intelligence is the ability to separate behaviors from the emotions surrounding them and identify, assess and control one's own emotions. As a simple example, displaying emotional intelligence might be taking a deep breath and saying, "I'm angry because any time someone compares me to my mother, it brings up some negative childhood experiences" rather than responding with a nasty comeback or violence.

- **Lack of courage** Coupled with a lack of communication skills, a lack of emotional courage can be devastating to a relationship. For intimacy to deepen over time, it's essential that the tough subjects be brought up and dealt with rather than avoided or swept under the rug. Lacking the courage to initiate difficult conversations is a key motivator for emotional distance and eventually, indifference. In order to keep a relationship healthy, one or more partners must have the strength and courage to face challenging issues. Fear points to where you should look, not in the direction you should run.

- **Fear of loss** Decisions made out of fear are rarely effective. If the only reason for staying in an unhealthy relationship is the fear of losing it, the relationship is already beyond saving. Occasionally, a partner will agree to try polyamory out of an explicit or implicit fear of losing the existing relationship if he/she isn't willing to trying opening up the relationship. Trying something new is great; trying something new because you're afraid your partner will leave you if you don't isn't.

Discovery Seven Summary

The most important factor in relationship success is you. Being a healthy, emotionally intelligent, happy individual and choosing a partner(s) who is also healthy, happy and emotionally intelligent are far better predictors of relationship success than anything else. Address any unresolved issues before dating, and be open to change.

DISCOVERY EIGHT

Change is good

I'm a big believer that life's challenges bring change, and those challenges that we overcome do change us for the better. Challenges show us who we are and what we are made of. They give us the opportunity to prove our strength to ourselves and our devotion to our partner(s). Challenges give us the chance to be the better person, to prove that we can handle being wrong and to revel in the joy that comes from unanticipated benefits.

Change is good. People change; opinions change; hobbies change; relationships change; goals change; life changes. Those who can embrace and accept change rather than fearing it tend to be happier in poly or any other relationship.

And in the words of one of my favorite poly pundits, Franklin Veaux, "Life rewards those who move in the direction of greatest courage." When confronted with frightening change, remember that you will be better off for having faced it than for running away. Regardless of the outcome of the relationship itself, you will be stronger and better for having faced change.

Conclusion

Whether you are new to poly, poly-curious or already in one or more poly relationships, I hope that these discoveries have been helpful to you. While it is my firm belief that each one of us crafts a relationship to fit our needs, it's also far too common for people to go about forming intimate relationships on their own, without ever seeking advice or support.

And whether you are monogamous, polyamorous or unsure of your orientation, there is no need for anyone to have to stumble through a new kind of relationship on their own. Resources abound, from books to blogs to real-life communities, and while not every resource might be to your liking, it is fortunate that these days, we have such a rich pool to choose from.

So do your self-assessment. Evaluate your current situation. Reach out and meet other poly folks. Learn your lessons; ask your questions and share your stories. Because it is also my belief that everyone has something valuable to offer to others, and we can all benefit from a bit more information.

Appendix

Writing your own user manual

This boilerplate serves as a guide for writing your own user manual, an excellent activity to showcase your self-awareness and communication skills. This is NOT a list of requirements or desires for dating or to "sell" yourself as you would on a dating profile but rather a pointed disclosure of your history, personality and emotional baggage.

A: Family background and history

This section is details not what you want but rather where you came from as a means of explaining your family ties (or lack thereof), norms and values.

- Do you have brothers and sisters? How would you characterize your relationship with them?
- How would you characterize your childhood and its effect on you now?
- What is your family like? How would you characterize your relationship with them?
- What word do you often use to describe yourself? Why?
- What word do others use to describe you? Do you think it's accurate?
- What are your key emotional issues a partner might bump into (anger, abuse, abandonment, name-calling, condescension)? Tell a story summarizing why they exist.
- What do you value in a relationship? Tell a story summarizing your embracing of that value.

B: How to turn me on emotionally

This section shares a few basics of how you operate on an emotional level. The goal is to lay out your emotional groundwork so a partner will be aware of your land mines.

- What small gestures carry extra meaning for you? Tell a story summarizing a small kindness that touched you. (Repeat as desired)
- What gestures increase intimacy for you? (reaching out in time of need, holding while you cry, etc.) Tell a story summarizing this gesture that was meaningful for you. (Repeat as desired)

- What kind of communication do you prefer? Tell a story of an instance of good communication.
- How do you react to conflict? How would you prefer a partner react?
- What is the best way for a partner to build trust with you?

C: How to turn me on

This section details some basics of flirting and your known sexual preferences. Share as much or as little as you are comfortable with. (Responses assume consent.)

- What is the best way to flirt with you?
- What kind of flirting will always get your attention and bring a smile?
- What kind of dates do you especially like?
- What kind of light physical touch do you enjoy?
- What does a good date look like to you? How would someone leave you walking away feeling that wonderful?
- Any particular flirting pet peeves to be avoided?
- What kind of pace do you prefer for dating/intimacy?
- What is "sex" to you?
- What are you into sexually?
- What is your take on casual sex?
- Why did you choose your last few sexual partners, and what did you enjoy about them?
- What are your known sexual turn-ons?
- What are your known sexual turn-offs?

Links

To view the links referenced in this book, visit http://polyweekly.com/eight-things-links/ or scan the QR code below:

ABOUT THE AUTHOR

Cunning Minx is the sultry-voiced producer and host of the Polyamory Weekly podcast, now with over 400 episodes in production. The free weekly podcast shares tales from the front of responsible non-monogamy from a pansexual, kink-friendly point of view. A kinky boobiesexual, Minx founded the show in 2005 as a resource for the poly and poly-curious to form community, share experiences and help guide each other on their journeys of poly and kinky exploration. The podcast is the longest-running polyamory podcast and winner of the 2007 Erotic Award for Best Podcast as well as receiving accolades from ErosZine, Fleshbot and the Chicago Sun-Times.

Minx has given dozens of lectures on polyamory, BDSM and social media activism at poly, kinky and science fiction conferences around the United States. She lives in Seattle with one decidedly grumpy old cat and enjoys salsa dancing and ass-boxing in her extremely limited free time. To book Minx to speak at your next conference, email cunningminx@gmail.com or to sign up to receive updates via email, visit http://eepurl.com/S1UID.

Made in the USA
Middletown, DE
15 February 2019